The World's Best Drinking Jokes

In this series:

The World's Best Dirty Jokes
More of the World's Best Dirty Jokes
Still More of the World's Best Dirty Jokes
The World's Best Irish Jokes
More of the World's Best Irish Jokes
Still More of the World's Best Irish Jokes
The World's Best Jewish Jokes
More of the World's Best Jewish Jokes
The World's Best Doctor Jokes
More of the World's Best Doctor Jokes
The World's Best Dirty Stories
The World's Best Dirty Limericks
The Word's Best Dirty Songs
The World's Best Aussie Jokes
The World's Best Catholic Jokes
The World's Best Mother-in-Law Jokes
The World's Best Russian Jokes
The World's Best Fishing Jokes
The World's Best Salesman Jokes
The World's Best Scottish Jokes
The World's Best Cricket Jokes
The World's Best Golf Jokes
More of the World's Best Golf Jokes
The World's Best Lawyer Jokes
The World's Best Business Jokes
The World's Best Holiday Jokes
The World's Best Acting Jokes
The World's Best Football Jokes
More of the World's Best Drinking Jokes
The World's Best Gardening Jokes
The World's Best Motoring Jokes
The World's Best Gambling Jokes
The World's Best Marriage Jokes

The World's Best Drinking Jokes

Ernest Forbes

Illustrated by

Neil Baker

HarperCollinsPublishers

HarperCollins*Publishers*
77–85 Fulham Palace Road,
Hammersmith, London W6 8JB

This paperback edition 1993
3 5 7 9 8 6 4 2

First published in Great Britain by
Angus & Robertson (UK) an imprint of
HarperCollins*Publishers* 1990

ISBN 0 00 638242 8

Set in Goudy Old Style

Printed in Great Britain by
HarperCollinsManufacturing Glasgow

A man walked into a Belfast pub and left a parcel on the bar. 'What's that?' asked the barman.
'It's my lunch.'
'Is it tickin'?'
'No, it's turkey.'

A man entered the same Belfast pub and handed the barman a sheet of paper and said: 'Make up that order for me.'

The barman read the list aloud, 'Twenty bottles of whisky, twenty bottles of brandy, twenty bottles of rum, twenty bottles of gin, twelve crates of beer, twelve crates of Guinness and a bottle of lemonade. Boy! That's some order and it'll cost you a bomb.'

'I know,' said the man, 'and that's it ticking on the counter.'

'Is there any alcohol in cider?'
'Inside whom?'

'I left a bottle of whisky in the train this morning.'
'Was it turned into the lost and found department?'
'No, but the man who found it was.'

Inspector: 'What made you think the man was drunk?'
Constable: 'He was having a heated argument with a taxi driver.'
Inspector: 'But that doesn't prove anything.'
Constable: 'Well, sir, there was no taxi driver.'

The drunk was trying to fit his door key into a street lamp as the policeman approached.

'I don't think there is anybody at home, sir,' said the policeman in a friendly tone.

'Mus' be offisher, mus' be. Theresh a light on upstairs.'

'Do you drink Guinness, Phil?'
'What else can you do with it?'

As the policeman helped the bruised and battered drunk up from the road in front of the pub, he asked, 'Can you describe the man who hit you?'

'Oh, yes,' said the drunk. 'That's just what I was doing when he hit me.'

He was so drunk by the time he left the pub and staggered to his car that he decided he couldn't even see the road. He watched another driver pulling away and decided to follow right behind him and be guided by his rear lights.

All went well for about five miles, when suddenly the

lights in front went out and the drunk rammed into the back of the other car with a sickening crunch. The drunk leaped out of his car.

'What the hell did you stop like that for?' he demanded.

'Why the hell shouldn't I?' growled the other driver. 'I'm in my own garage.'

'Drink,' said the Irish preacher, 'is the greatest curse known to man. It makes you quarrelsome and it makes you angry with your wife. It makes you want to shoot your wife – and it makes you miss.'

'Trade's bad, Paddy, I think I'll sell the pub and start a brothel.'

'Won't work, Mike. If you can't sell beer what makes you think you could sell soup?'

The host was well known for his stinginess. At a party he told everybody that he had a prize crate of Napoleon brandy and offered every guest a sample. An old hand took up the offer and got about three drops deposited in his glass.

'How old did you say this brandy was?' he asked.

'Over a hundred and fifty years old,' replied the host.

The man sniffed and looked at the glass. 'Bit small for its age,' he observed.

The barman looked up casually from wiping the counter as two pink elephants marched into the pub.

'Sorry, chaps,' said the barman with a smile, 'but Michael hasn't been in this evening.'

The social worker knocked on the door which was opened by Mrs O'Toole.

'Good evening. I'm collecting for a home for drunkards,' said the caller. 'Would you care to make a donation?'

'I certainly would,' replied Mrs O'Toole. 'Come back after the pubs shut and I'll give you my husband.'

A drunk approached a policeman and asked, 'Offisher, where's the other side of the street?'

'That's it over there,' pointed the policeman.

'I thought as much. Some wise guy told me this is it.'

A drunk staggered into the reception area of The Hollywood Roosevelt Hotel and said to the desk clerk, 'I'd like the key to room 555, please.'

'I'm sorry, sir,' said the clerk, 'but that room is occupied.'

'Not now it isn't,' replied the drunk, 'I just fell out of the window.'

A motorist was stopped by a traffic patrol and informed by the sergeant he had been travelling at ninety miles per hour.

'Nothing of the sort, sergeant,' snorted the man, 'I was only doing fifty.'

'You were doing ninety.'

'I tell you I was doing fifty,' shouted the man.

At which point his wife interjected, 'No use arguing with him officer. He's always like this when he's had a few drinks.'

Then there is the sad story about the drunk who was badly bitten. He went home one night sober and his dog didn't recognise him.

Doctor: 'Do you realise that every drink you take shortens your life by a month?'

Patient: 'That can't be right, doctor, otherwise I would have been dead for the last twenty years.'

Sad news about the man who died from drinking varnish. He had a terrible end, but a beautiful finish.

The drunk staggered into the pub and ordered a round of drinks for everyone in the place.

'And make sure the barman has one,' he insisted.

After the drinks were served the barman presented the man with a bill for £22 and was hopping mad when the drunk announced that he hadn't a penny on him. The barman threw the drunk out of the pub on to the pavement.

The very next night the drunk staggered in again, ordered a drink for everyone in the pub and slapped two £20 notes on the counter.

'Only don't give that miserable barman a drink. Give him one drop and he turns violent.'

'Every time I get drunk I see hundreds of green snakes in my dreams,' confided Ray to his friend.

'Have you seen a doctor?' asked his friend anxiously.

'No, only green snakes.'

'Waiter – hic – bring me a dish of prunes.'

'Stewed, sir?'

'Thash none of your bishness.'

First Drunk: 'Hey, barman, gimmie a horse's neck.'

Second Drunk: 'I'll have a horse's tail. No bloody need to kill two horses.'

The Irishman had to tell Mrs Murphy the sad news about her husband, who had died by drowning in a large vat of beer at the brewery.

'Tell me, did he die quickly and painlessly?' she asked.

'Painless, certainly,' said the man, 'but quickly, no. In fact, it wasn't until the third time that we pulled him out that we realised he was starting to drown.'

The drunk tottered into his home and asked, 'Is that bottle of brown stuff in the bathroom, shampoo?'

'No, it's glue,' answered his wife.

'Christ, no wonder I couldn't get my hat off in the pub,' muttered the drunk.

The telephone rang in the office of Alcoholics Anonymous at midnight.

'I need help,' said a drunken voice on the telephone. 'At this moment I am sitting in a room surrounded by forty bottles of wine.'

'How can we help,' asked the AA man.

'I thought you might be able to put me in touch with one of your members who might have a corkscrew he's not using any more,' said the man.

Two judges got drunk and were arrested for drunken behaviour and each agreed to try the other's case.

The first judge came into court and pleaded guilty. His friend fined him five pounds. Then it was his turn to judge his companion.

'I sentence you to thirty days in prison,' he said.

His friend was astonished and exclaimed, 'But I only fined you five pounds.'

'I know,' said the second judge. 'But there's too much of this sort of thing. This is the second case I've heard today.'

The Irishman walked into an English pub and ordered eighteen pints of beer.

'Have you a party outside?' asked the barman.

'No, they're for me.'

'Eighteen pints?' questioned the barman.

'Well it's your ruling,' said the Irishman pointing to a sign over the bar – NOBODY SERVED UNDER EIGHTEEN.

Two sailors, retiring from the sea, bought a pub in a small village. They closed it for redecoration but as time passed the villagers grew impatient at the closure. One day a number of the villagers went to the pub and hammered on the door. After some time a window was opened and one of the men looked out.

'Whash you want?' he slurred.

'We want to know when you are going to open the pub,' one of the villagers shouted.

'Open the pub? Open the pub?' replied the man. 'Who's shaid we were going to open? We bought this place for ourselves.'

Why has a glass of Guinness a white head on it? So an Irishman knows which end to drink first.

The two drunks met in the pub.

'Sad times,' said one drunk.

'Indeed,' agreed the second.

'I buried my wife today.'

'That's sad,' sympathised the second. 'But I thought you buried your wife six months ago.'

'I did, but I remarried.'

'Congratulations,' said the second drunk lifting his glass.

'Thanks,' said the first drunk.

The drunk was sitting in the corner of a bar, holding an empty glass and sobbing quietly.

'What's the matter?' asked the barman.

'I did a terrible thing yesterday,' sobbed the drunk. 'I sold my wife to a stranger for a bottle of Scotch.'

'And now you want her back again,' said the barman softly.

'Yes,' whispered the drunk. 'Oh, yes.'

'You want her back because you realise how much you love her,' prompted the barman.

'Oh, no,' answered the drunk. 'I want her back because I'm thirsty again.'

Policeman: 'Excuse me, sir, do you know who I am?'

Drunk: 'I can't shay ash I do, but if you tell me where you live I'll help you home.'

'How did you get those scars on the top of your nose?'

'From glasses.'

'Why don't you try contact lenses?'

'They don't hold enough beer.'

'Excuse me, I'm a stranger here. Where's the nearest boozer?'

'You're looking at him.'

The doctor was very plain in his warning to the heavy drinker.

'If you keep drinking at your present rate you will be dead in five years,' said the doctor waving a warning finger. 'I suggest you cut down to only five drinks a day.'

The man agreed to take his advice and left.

Two weeks later the doctor met the man in the street and the man was blind drunk.

The doctor was very angry, 'I thought I told you only five drinks.'

'Yes, doctor,' replied the drunk. 'I took your advice but then I went to three other doctors for second opinions – and they all prescribed five drinks as well.'

The painter fell off the ladder and was lying on the pavement. The foreman rushed up and shouted, 'This man has just fallen ten feet, get him a glass of water.'

The painter eased himself up on one elbow and asked, 'How far do I have to fall to get a glass of whisky?'

The drunk was asked why he was walking with one foot on the pavement and the other in the gutter.

'Is that what I'm doing?' he replied. 'Thank God – I thought one leg was shorter than the other.'

Then there was the Irish farmer who gave his chickens whisky every day in the hope they would lay Scotch eggs.

Three drunks left the pub and took a taxi to the railway station, arriving just as the train was about to leave.

A helpful porter managed to get two of them aboard and apologised to the man left behind.

'I'm sorry I couldn't get you on the train, sir,' he said.

'So am I,' said the drunk, 'because my pals were only here to see me off.'

The drunk was crawling about the pavement under a streetlight.

'Looking for something, sir?' asked a policeman.

'My wallet, offisher, I dropped my wallet.'

'Exactly where did you drop it?'

'In the other street.'

'Well, why are you searching for it here?'

'Because it's too bloody dark round there.'

As a drunk lurched down the road he saw a motorist looking under the bonnet of his car.

'Whash the matter?'

'Piston broke,' came the reply.

'Me too,' slurred the drunk staggering off.

Edward Carson, the famous Irish advocate, was cross-examining a hostile witness.

'You drink, don't you?' he enquired.

'That's my business,' growled the witness.

'Have you any other business?' asked Carson and sat down.

Barrister (to witness): 'You say the defendant was drunk.'
Witness: 'Yes, sir, drunk as a judge.'
Judge: 'You mean drunk as a lord?'
Witness: 'Yes, my lord.'

Two drunks were staggering home one night. One looked up and asked, 'Is that the sun or the moon up there?'

'Dunno,' replied the other. 'I don't live around here.'

The big preacher was in full flow and he shouted, 'Name me one thing that is worse than drink.'

'Thirst,' came the reply from the back of the hall.

The barman watched the drunk search all his pockets before he found his car keys. The barman whispered to the drunk, 'Sir, why don't you take a taxi home?'

'Sh no ushe, George,' said the drunk. 'My wife wouldn't let me keep it in the houshe.'

'Jack was held up on the way home last night.'
'That's the only way he could have got home.'

'Was your father drunk when he came home last night, Elizabeth?'
'I don't think so mother, but he did ask for a mirror to see who he was.'

The drunk was staggering along the street when he saw a little boy sitting on a step crying.
'What's the matter, little boy?' said the drunk kindly.
'I can't do what the big boys do,' sobbed the little boy.
'Neither can I,' said the drunk. 'But the cure for brewer's droop is unthinkable.'

A drunk was swaying back and forth on the pavement when a policeman asked him what he was doing and where he lived.
'Right there,' said the drunk pointing to a house. 'I rang the bell but nobody answered.'
'How long ago was that?'
'Bout three hours.'
'Well, why don't you try them again?'
'Aw, to hell with them – let them wait.'

The intoxicated diner beckoned the waiter over to his table.

'Waiter, I feel I have had too much to drink. Will you please bring me something to sober me up quickly.'

'Certainly, sir, I'll get your bill.'

What did your husband die of?'

'Love.'

'Oh, I heard a rumour that he died of drink.'

'That's right – he died of love of drink.'

A drunk staggered into a shopping mall and made his way to the sweet counter.

'Do you,' he gurgled, 'do you sell those – lic – er – lic – liqueur chocolates with brandy in the middle?'

'Yes, we do,' said the assistant.

'Good,' chirped the drunk. 'Give me five pounds of middles.'

Man: 'Do you serve women in this bar?'

Barman: 'No, you have to bring your own.'

A man helped his drunken friend into a nearby hotel, having decided that he was in no fit condition to go home.

'I'm afraid you can't bring him in here,' said the receptionist, 'this is a temperance hotel.'

'Oh, don't worry about that,' said the man. 'He's far too drunk to notice.'

'You know,' said the Irishman as he downed his drink, 'one swallow does not make a summer.'

'True,' agreed the American, 'but several swallows frequently make a fall.'

Pat: 'Do you drink alone?'
Mike: 'Not unless I'm with someone.'

The two men planned to go fishing. 'I'll bring the fishing gear,' said one, 'and you bring the provisions.'

The provisions man arrived with one loaf of bread and four bottles of whisky.

'Fine thing,' snapped the gear man. 'I leave the provisions to you and what do you bring? One loaf of bread and four bottles of booze, now what the hell are we going to do with all that bread?'

The drunk staggered up to the hotel reception and demanded his room be changed.

'But sir,' said the clerk, 'you have the best room in the hotel.'

'I insist on another room,' said the drunk.

'Very good sir. I'll change you from 502 to 555.'

'Shank you,' slurred the man.

'Would you mind telling me why you don't like 502?' asked the clerk.

'Well, for one thing,' said the drunk, 'it's on fire.'

When the fight broke out in the pub old Sam was knocked about.

'Did you get hit in the fracas?' asked a young policeman.

'No, officer,' said Sam, 'in the eye.'

When Dean Martin was told that whisky killed more people than bullets, the star replied, 'That may be true – but I'd rather be full of whisky than full of bullets.'

The late Errol Flynn claimed it only took one drink to get him drunk but he couldn't remember if it was the 18th or 19th.

'Tell me, what are those pigeons doing on your head?'

'I don't know,' slurred the drunk. 'They just got on at Trafalgar Square.'

The husband came down to breakfast with a helluva hangover.

'What was all that screaming about last night?' asked his wife.

'I had a terrible dream or maybe I should call it a hellish nightmare,' replied her husband holding his head on. 'I dreamed that someone shot me and when I woke up and looked in the mirror there was a big hole in my head.'

'What happened then?' asked his wife.

'It went away when I closed my mouth.'

Then there was the barman in Glasgow who considered it an insult if a customer bought him a drink. However, he was a sensible lad and soon learned to swallow the insults.

The drunk beckoned to the barmaid.

'A large – hic – hic – a large cigar and a packet of peanuts please,' he requested.

'I didn't know you liked peanuts,' said the girl.

'Don't,' replied the drunk with a knowing nod. 'They're for my little friend, the pink elephant here.'

The publican was pleased when a man who owed him for a round of drinks came into the bar one morning.

'About that money I owe you ...' began the man.

'I haven't given it a second thought,' the publican lied.

The customer sat on a stool and ordered a large brandy which he quickly drank. Then he stood up.

'Glad you're not worried about the money, because that makes it an even tenner I owe you now,' he said and walked out of the pub.

It was getting near closing time and the barman suggested to Charles, who was 'not feeling any pain', that he should go home for his supper.

'Why should I?' demanded Charles. 'All I'll get is hot tongue and cold shoulder.'

The Irishman wanted to go back to Ireland but was £1 short of his fare so he walked into a London pub and asked in a loud voice, 'Has anybody here got a £1 to send a poor homesick Irishman back to the land of his fathers.'

'Shertainly,' said a happy drunk sitting at the bar. 'Here's £20, take another nineteen with you.'

Wife: 'Darling, will you give up drinking for
            me?'
Husband: 'Who said I was drinking for you?'

A drunk guest embraced a strange woman at a party. 'Excuse me, madam, but I thought you were my wife,' he mumbled apologetically as he realised his mistake.

'You're a fine husband to have,' said the irate lady, 'just look at you, you're a clumsy, drunken, disgusting brute.'

Good heavens!' exclaimed the drunk. 'Not only do you look like my wife, you talk just like here, too.'

The customer was lighting a cigarette and the barman said, 'You're a stranger here, aren't you sir?'

'Yes I am. How did you know?'

'You just put your drink down.'

The sales manager of a large company approached one of his salesmen at the bar and said, 'If you didn't drink so much, you could be sales manager of this company instead of me. Doesn't that make you think that it would be worthwhile staying sober?'

'Not at all,' replied the salesman. 'When I'm drunk I'm the managing director.'

A drunk walked into a bar and asked, 'Was I in here last night?'

'Yes, you were,' replied the barman.

'Did I spend much money?' asked the drunk.

'About £80,' said the barman.

The drunk breathed a sigh of relief, and said, 'Thank God! I thought I'd lost it.'

Two friends left a pub after a heavy drinking session, and staggered through Piccadilly Circus. Suddenly one of them disappeared down the underground entrance without a word. The next night the two men met again and the first drunk asked his friend where he had ended up.

'Well,' said the second drunk, 'I went to see a friend who lives in a basement flat and boy, you really ought to see his train set!'

A drunk on a bus was tearing up a newspaper into small pieces and throwing them out of the window.

'Excuse me,' said the man sitting next to him, 'why are you tearing up that paper and throwing the pieces out of the window?'

'To scare away the elephants,' said the drunk.

'I don't see any elephants,' said the man.

'Effective, isn't it?' smiled the drunk.

'What does your husband do for a living?'

'He's a joiner.'

'Oh yes? What does he do?'

'Whenever he sees someone going into a pub he joins them.'

'What's that drink you're mixing?' the man asked the girl behind the bar.

'I call this a brandy dandy,' replied the girl.

'What's in it?' asked the drinker.

'Sugar, milk and brandy.'

'Is it good?' asked the man.

'Sure is,' answered the girl. 'The sugar gives you pep and the milk gives you energy.'

'And the brandy?' enquired the man.

'Ideas about what to do with all that pep and energy.'

A polished drinker is a man who opens a bottle of whisky and throws the cork into the fireplace.

Men often make passes at girls who drain glasses.

'Sorry I'm late, dear, but I was competing in a beer-drinking contest at the pub,' said the happy husband.

'Oh, really?' said his wife coldly. 'And who came second?'

A cowboy walks into a saloon, bangs on the bar and orders a whisky. He drinks the whisky, whips round and shoots a nick in the ear lobe of the pianist. The barman advises him to file his sights off. So he files off the sights and orders another whisky. Drinks it quickly, swings round and shoots a nick in the other ear of the pianist.

'Why don't you grease the barrel?' said the barman. 'It'll be better if you grease the barrel.'

'Why will it be better with no sights and a greased barrel?' asked the cowboy.

'Cos when Wyatt Earp has finished playing the piano, he's gonna shove that gun right up your arse.'

'Well, another night spent drinking in the pub. What's the excuse this time?' demanded the wife.

'Well, there I was, drink in hand, in front of a blazing fire. It was very difficult to leave.'

'Why didn't you get up and walk away?'

'I couldn't get past all those firemen and their equipment,' replied the husband.

After finishing his fifth double whisky the drunk slammed his fist on the bar and shouted, 'Everybody on the right side of this bar is a bastard.'

The crowd ignored him.

Angered the drunk continued, 'Everybody on the left side of the bar is a gay.'

Again, there was silence until a young man got up and walked across the room.

'So,' challenged the drunk, 'you want to fight?'

'Certainly not,' replied the young man. 'Just that I'm on the wrong side of the room.'

'If your wife is so beautiful, why do you get drunk every night?' asked the first drunk.

'So I can see two of her,' replied the second drunk.

The affable drunk was tottering along the street pulling a piece a string.

'Why are you pulling the string?' asked a friendly policeman.

'Shay, offisher, have you ever tried pushing a piece of string?' swayed the drunk.

The two terrorists each had a few drinks before setting out on a bombing mission. They got into the car and the passenger placed a bomb on his lap.

'I better – hic – not drive too fast – hic –,' said the driver, 'or the bomb you're carrying might – hic – go off.'

'Doesn't matter,' slurred the passenger. 'Go as fast as you like, there's another one in the boot.'

The wedding reception was being held in the top executive suite of a hotel. One of the guests, very much the worse for drink, asked the way to the toilet.

After getting directions the drunk set off to find the place. In his drunken state, however, he managed to walk into the lift shaft and fell ten floors. As he hit the ground he looked up and shouted in alarm, 'For Christ's sake, nobody flush the toilet until I get out.'

Then there was the elephant who drank so much he started to see pink people.

'I'm bringing my son up to be like me. His schoolteacher asked him the meaning of the word "straight" and he answered, "Without soda".'

He was trying to soften up the girl's resistance with drink, but she flatly refused; she insisted she had never touched a drop in her life. Finally he had the lights down low and the soft music playing and he had persuaded her to try a drop of Scotch. The girl took a little sip and then spat it out in disgust.

'Don't you like the taste?' he asked.

'No, I don't,' said the girl. 'You said Scotch and then you give me Irish whisky and a cheap one at that.'

Then there was the drunk motorist who was stopped for speeding. He explained to the policeman that he felt he was too drunk to drive safely, so he was hurrying home before he caused an accident.

The man dashed into the pub and whispered to the barman, 'Give me a drink, quickly – before the row starts.'

As the barman pulled the pint the customer looked out of the window. He drank the pint and had another look out into the street.

'There's still time. Give me another one before the row starts.'

When he was halfway down the second pint, the barman asked, 'What's the trouble, anyway? What row is going to start?'

'It'll be any minute now. I've no money.'

As he poured her a drink he said, 'Say when.'
'After this drink,' she replied.

Acute alcoholic is a pretty drunk.

When Michael O'Toole died, they gave him a wonderful funeral. It took six strong men to carry the beer.

The party was over, but a few of the heavy drinkers were still hanging around when a fire broke out. The host shouted to all his guests in a drunken voice, 'There's only one chance, we must jump out of the window.'
'But we're on the thirteenth floor,' one of the guests protested.
'This is no time to be bloody superstitious,' snorted the host.

Patrick O'Flynn, who appeared in a London Court on a charge of being drunk and disorderly claimed it was his doctor's fault. O'Flynn stated he had telephoned his doctor to ask for treatment for a corn on the sole of his foot. The doctor had said he was too busy and told O'Flynn to treat himself, which he had done by buying eight pints, two rums and an Irish Coffee.

In a London Court a police officer stated that the defendant was drunk and tried to drink directly from a bottle.

The defending barrister immediately asked, 'Then in your opinion it is proof of drunkenness to drink the contents directly from a bottle?'

'Well, sir,' replied the police officer, 'in this case I would say yes as the bottle contained a model of a three masted ship.'

Mary: 'What's your favourite drink?'
Sean: 'The next one.'

First Drunk: 'Do you know what time it is?'
Second Drunk: 'Yes.'
First Drunk: 'Thanks.'

One should never drink on an empty stomach.
Be wise – have a couple of beers first.

Then there were the two old Scotsmen who bumped into each other after 40 years and immediately went into the nearest pub to celebrate.

'Won't it be nice to drink to our reunion?' said one.

'Yes it will,' agreed the other. 'But don't forget it's your round, I bought the drinks the last time.'

An Irishman who appeared in court pleaded not guilty to a charge of drunken driving. He claimed that after he and his three friends left an all night party he was too drunk to sing so he had to drive.

Denis: 'Drink makes you look very beautiful and sexy.'
Margaret: 'But I haven't been drinking.'
Denis: 'No, but I have.'

In London today an Irish laundryman was found guilty of being drunk and disorderly but was given a suspended sentence on condition that in future he would be a dry cleaner.

A drunk staggered up to the owner of a pub and shook a finger at him.

'I want to complain about your barman in the lounge upstairs,' panted the drunk.

'What happened?' asked the owner.

'He kicked my hat down the stairs, that's what he did,' protested the drunk.

'Probably having a little joke, surely you don't mind that?' coaxed the owner.

'Well, I do mind,' insisted the drunk. 'I was wearing the hat at the time.'

'What are you doing?'
    'I'm trying to make a case for beer.'
'You don't need to – I'm convinced.'

The drunk was staggering down the street at two o'clock in the morning. A police car drew alongside him.
    'Where are you going?' asked a policeman.
    'Shay, offisher, I'm going to a lecture.'
    'A lecture at this time of night?'
    'Shertainly.'
    'Who's giving it?'
    'My wife.'

A policeman observed an Irishman sitting in a lay-by throwing empty beer cans out of the car window.
    'What do you think you're doing?' asked the policeman.
    'I'm on the works outing.'
    'But you're alone.'
    'I know,' said the Irishman. 'I'm self-employed.'

'My wife said she would leave me if I didn't stop drinking.'
    'Oh, I am sorry.'
    'Me too, I'm going to miss her.'

Show me a man at a bottle party who can eat, drink and be merry – and I'll show you a fat, grinning drunk.

The two drunks were on a fishing holiday in Florida and while happily fishing from a dock one drunk cried out in pain.

'An alligator has just bitten off my toe.'

'Which one?' yelled his companion.

'How the hell do I know – all alligators look the same to me.'

'Mum! Here comes dad, holding a policeman on each arm!'

The couple, celebrating their wedding anniversary, had quite a few drinks, bought a bottle of champagne and headed for the Grand Opera House where they had booked seats.

The girl in the foyer took their tickets and enquired if they wanted glasses.

'No, thanks,' said the man, pulling the champagne from his pocket, 'we'll drink it straight from the bottle.'

Mick was in court for being drunk and disorderly. When the magistrate found out that he was unemployed, he wanted to know where he got the money for the drink.

'My friend, Hamish McTavish, bought all the drink,' explained Mick.

'Two months imprisonment for perjury,' snapped the magistrate.

Then there was the Irishman who was drunk and fell into an open grave on his way home from a drinking session. He promptly fell asleep. He woke up the next morning and looked at his surroundings.

'Holy mackerel,' he cried. 'It's Judgement Day and I'm the only one up!'

The two men had imbibed rather freely in the pub during the morning and as they staggered through the cemetery a funeral service was taking place. From the graveside floated the words of the minister, '... and now we put to rest a politician and a honest man.'

'S'funny,' muttered one drunk. 'Didn't know they were allowed to bury two men in the same coffin.'

There are two kinds of people at most parties; those who want to leave early and those who don't. Trouble is they're usually married to each other.

Patient: 'Doctor, I keep thinking I'm a bottle of gin.'
Doctor: 'What you need is a little tonic.'

A drunk asked a woman the way to Alcoholics Anonymous.

'Do you wish to join?' enquired the woman.
'No,' was the reply, 'to resign.'

A beautiful young blonde walked into the bar and ordered a Campari and soda.

'How old are you, miss?' asked the barman.

'Sixteen,' replied the girl.

'Then you've had it,' said the barman.

'I know,' smiled the girl, 'that's what made me so thirsty.'

A horse trotted into a pub and ordered a pint of beer. He put £5 on the bar and the barman gave him £1 change. As he served the drink the barman said, 'Excuse me for mentioning it but we don't get many horses in here.'

'I'm not surprised,' said the horse, 'with beer at £4 a pint.'

'Everyone have a drink,' shouted the man as he entered the pub. 'When I drink, everybody has to drink.'

The barman served everyone in the pub with a free drink.

The generous man raised his glass, 'Everybody be happy. When I'm happy, everybody has to be happy.'

Draining his glass the man left £1 on the bar counter and started to leave.

'That's only enough for your own drink,' pointed out the barman.

'That's right,' said the man. 'When I pay, everybody has to pay.'

The man walked into a pub and stepped over the inert body of a drunk who lay on the floor.

'What will you have?' asked the barman.

The customer pointed to the body of the drunk, 'I'll have what he had.'

It was Christmas party time and the police car driver stopped a car to congratulate the driver on his driving.

'I wish all drivers were like you sir. You observed the speed limit, displayed care, caution and consideration,' said the police officer.

'Well, offisher,' came the reply, 'you've got to watch it when you've had a few.'

A drunk stopped a man and asked if he had any loose change for a cup of coffee.

The man gave the drunk a fiver with the remark, 'Have six cups.'

Next day, the drunk stopped the man again and complained, 'You and your six cups of coffee. Bloody well sobered me up.'

The two drunks met in the bar.

'What's the date, Sammy?' asked one.

'Dunno,' replied Sammy.

'Well, look at the newspaper in your pocket.'

'No use,' said Sammy. 'It's yesterday's.'

A drunken man lurched into a pub near closing time and ordered a pint.

Suddenly, overcome by the amount he had consumed, he was sick all over a little dog by the bar.

Looking down he muttered, 'I can't remember eating that.'

The social worker rubbed her chin thoughtfully and said, 'It would appear to me you have a drinking problem.'

'I haven't a drinking problem,' retorted the man. 'I go out to drink. Get drunk. Pass out. Get carried home. So what's the problem?'

'Here comes The Exorcist,' said the barman as a man entered the pub.

'Why do you call him that?' asked the new assistant barman.

'Because he can move more spirits than anyone I know.'

Three drunks stagger into a pub near closing time. One collapses in a heap on the floor. The others order a brandy each.

'What about him?' asked the barman indicating the bundle on the floor.

'No more for him,' said one man, 'he'sh driving.'

'When my husband gets drunk he thinks he's a purple rhinoceros.'

'Is that bad?'

'Well, he keeps charging Land Rovers.'

It was a thick, foggy night in Belfast as the drunk lurched out of a city centre pub. He eventually found a nearby taxi rank.

'Could you take me to Cherryvalley?' asked the drunk politely.

'Sorry, sir,' said the driver, 'but I'm not going to move until this fog lifts.'

'I'll pay you double the fare,' offered the drunk, 'I've just got to get home or my wife will kill me.'

The driver thought about this for a moment then he made the drunk an offer.

'Pay me treble the fare, and I'll go and get one of the other drivers to walk in front of the taxi with a red torch,' he suggested.

'Shertainly not,' slurred the drunk. 'Give me the torch and I'll walk in front.'

Judge: 'Do you recognise this court?'
Drunk: 'Not since it's been decorated.'

An optimist says a bottle of whisky is half full. A pessimist says it's half empty.

One of the drunks looked very secretive as he cupped his hands.

'Guess what I have in my hands,' he said to his drinking companion.

'A television set.'

'No – have another guess.'

'A horse.'

'No – try again.'

'A beautiful blonde.'

The first drunk burst into tears, 'That's not fair – you peeked.'

What do you drink?'

'Brandy and carrot juice.'

'Funny mixture.'

'Well, you get drunk just as fast and you can see where you're going to fall.'

She was awakened by a tremendous crash and dashing downstairs saw their car in the dining room.

'How did you get the car in the dining room?' she cried to her drunken husband who was sitting in the driving seat.

'Seasy,' slurred her husband. 'I made a left turn when I came out of the kitchen.'

'There's only one hope for you,' said the doctor. 'You will have to give up drinking for a year.'

The patient was appalled, 'But doctor, if I give up drinking for a year I'll have a nervous breakdown.'

'Sure you will,' agreed the doctor, 'but think of all the money you'll have saved to pay the hospital expenses.'

It was dawn and the Mexican bandit was facing the firing squad. He let the officer place a blindfold over his eyes and turned down the offer of a cigarette.

'I would like a glass of water,' said the bandit.

'Are you sure you wouldn't rather have a shot of Tequila?' said the officer.

'No thanks, water will be fine,' replied the bandit. 'I'm trying to give up alcohol.'

I must have a drink of breakfast.'

W.C. Fields

Nigel and Basil were very drunk as they staggered home by way of the river. Basil slipped and fell in the river. Considering his state Nigel quickly pulled him out.

At two in the morning a policeman knocked on Nigel's door.

'Did you rescue Basil Browning from the river last night?' asked the policeman.

'Yesh, I did offisher,' replied the still inebriated Nigel.

'Well, I'm sorry to tell you he's hanged himself from a tree.'

'Ish that shoo? I jest put him there to dry.'

Two drunks staggering along the street came to a bus garage.

'Let's pinch a bus and get home,' said the first drunk.

'We'll never get ours out – it's right at the back,' said the other.

The two men were sitting in the snug, drinking their pints and discussing their amorous activities.

'My wife has no time for oral sex,' said one.

'That so? Well, my wife doesn't mind talking about sex at all,' replied the other man.

He had just returned from a visit to the doctor.

'What did the doctor say?' asked his wife.

'He says I'm suffering from syncopation,' replied the husband and went quickly upstairs.

'Oh, dear,' said the worried wife not knowing what it was. She checked the dictionary to find, Syncopation: An uneven progress from bar to bar.

'Drink! for you know not whence you came, nor why: Drink! for you know not why you go, nor where.'

Omar Khayyám

As he was leaving the pub the drunk bought a bottle of cheap red wine and stuck it in his pocket. As he was staggering down the road he tripped and fell into the gutter. As he picked himself up, he noticed a dark red stain spreading across the pavement.

He raised his eyes to heaven, 'Please let it be blood.'

The drunk rushed up the stairs to the fifth floor of a building and threw himself out of a window. A crowd gathered around him as he lay on the pavement.

A policeman dashed to the spot and knelt beside the man, 'What happened?'

'Don't ask me,' said the drunk. 'I only just got here myself.'

The doctor finished his examination, shook his head with puzzlement and turned to his patient.

'I can't find anything wrong with you, Mr Flynn. I can only assume it must be heavy drinking.'

'That's fine, doctor,' said Mr Flynn cheerfully, 'I'll come back when you're sober.'

The husband staggered into his house and was greeted by his angry wife.

'Drunk again!' she exclaimed. 'I see you walked home and had the good sense not to drive.'

'Couldn't get the car started.'

'What's the matter with it?'

'There's water in the carburettor.'

'Where is the car?'
'In the river.'

Patient: 'Doctor, if I stop drinking, will I live longer?'
Doctor: 'Probably not, it'll just seem longer.'

He was a compulsive drinker. If there was a nip in the air he'd try and drink it.

The barman froze when he saw the ghosts standing at the bar on the stroke of midnight.
'Do you,' said one ghost, 'serve spirits at this time of night?'

The husband was telephoning from the pub, 'I know I said I'd be home after six, but I haven't finished my fourth yet.'

'Hey, barman,' slurred the unpleasant drunk, 'do you know how to make a Hawaiian Flip?'
'Certainly, sir,' replied the barman. 'Set fire to her grass skirt.'

The drunk entered the pub and carefully made his way to the bar and held onto it in a studied fashion. He beckoned to the barman and asked, 'Seen Billy 'bout here 'n the lash hour?'

'Yes, he was here.'

'Ja notice if I was with him?'

Wife: 'You were drunk last night.'
Husband: 'What makes you say that?'
Wife: 'You were trying to get your trousers off over your head.'

Doctor: 'How long have you been on the wagon?'
Patrick: 'In twenty-nine days' time it will be a month.'

'Have you seen Anthony Hopkins as Titus Andronicus?'
'I don't know. How tight does Andronicus get?'

Sign outside a pub on the Belfast-Dublin Road: LAST PUB TILL THE NEXT ONE.

First Drunk: 'I don't have a lovelife.'
Second Drunk: 'How come?'
First Drunk: 'Well, every night my wife has a headache and every morning I have a hangover.'

The man dashed into the pub and joined his friend at the bar gasping, 'Can't stay very long, Jack, my wife thinks I'm having a shower.'

Ted: 'Every time I get a bad cold I buy a bottle of whisky, and take it home. Within an hour it's completely gone.'

Paul: 'What, the cold?'

Ted: 'No, the whisky.'

At two o'clock in the morning the publican was wakened by the telephone. The caller was one of his regulars, Terry Downe.

'Hey, what time do you open in the morning?' asked Terry.

'Eleven o'clock,' snapped the irate publican and put the telephone down.

Three hours later, the telephone rang and once again it was Terry.

'What time did you say you opened the pub in the morning?' questioned Terry.

'I told you eleven o'clock,' shouted the angry publican. 'I can tell you right now I won't let you in a minute before that.'

'I don't want to be let in,' said Terry. 'I want to be let out.'

The patient held out his hands and said, 'Look, doctor, my hands won't stop shaking.'

Looking at the hands the doctor asked, 'Do you drink much?'

'No,' replied the patient, 'I spill most of it.'

'Somebody left the cork out of my lunch.'

W.C. *Fields*

The temperance preacher tried a new approach to the evils of drink. Instead of appealing to his congregation on medical and religious grounds, he hit out at the financial aspect.

'Don't you realise who you give all your money to,' he said. 'The publican, that's who. Who is always rich? Who drives a big flashy car? Who buys his wife mink coats? The publican, that's who.'

A year later he was back in the same town and a well dressed man rushed up to him and shook his hand.

'Preacher, I want to thank you from the bottom of my heart,' said the man. 'Last year when you were here I listened to your lecture and it changed my way of life. I gave up drinking and took your advice. Today I'm a healthy, happy and wealthy man.'

'I'm glad I was able to help you,' said the temperance preacher. 'What are you doing now?'

'I own three pubs,' said the man proudly.

'Ish this Wembley?' asked the first drunk.
'No, Thursday,' answered the second drunk.
'So am I – le'sh have a drink,' said the third drunk.

Two drunks out walking got separated. Said one to a policeman, 'I say, ossifer, have you seen another man walking about without me?'

A drunk staggered into Alcoholics Anonymous, tripped and fell to the floor.
'Oh, Mr Black, when you turned up sober last time, you made me so very happy,' said the pretty young secretary.
'Well, dear,' hiccuped the drunk, 'tonight it's my turn to be happy.'

Barman on the telephone: 'Lady, this bar is packed with good-for-nothing, lazy, drunken and layabout husbands. You'll have to give me a better description than that.'

A drunk stopped a taxi, got in, fell out of the other door, picked himself up, and turning to the driver asked, 'How mush?'

'**W**hy do you think this man was inebriated?' asked the inspector.

'Well, sir,' replied the police constable, 'I found him in Trafalgar Square, throwing his umbrella in the fountain and trying to get one of the stone lions to fetch it.'

Two men tottered out of a country pub and up a lane. Some distance up the lane one man side stepped to avoid a cow standing in the road but the other man walked into it. The collision knocked him on his back.

His friend looked at him and gasped, 'Bloody hell. Didn't you see the cow?'

'Yes,' came the reply, 'but I didn't think it was real.'

A man entered a pub and was approached by a customer who asked, 'Are you Dr Thompson?'

'No,' was the reply.

'How strange, then you must have a double.'

'Thank you, I will,' said the man.

He was too drunk to drive so one of his friends put him in a taxi. When they arrived at the street the driver asked, 'What's the number of your house?'

'Don't arsk shilly questions,' said the reveller, 'itsh on the door.'

The man slid gently and rather gracefully from the bar stool and ended in a drunken heap on the floor.

'What's your name, and I'll tell your wife,' said the helpful barman.

'Thank you,' hiccuped the man, 'but my wife knows my name.'

Paddy Murphy stood before the magistrate.

'You again?' grunted the magistrate.

'Yes, sor,' replied Paddy.

'Who brought you here?' asked the magistrate.

'Two policemen, sor.'

'Drunk I suppose?'

'Yes, sor, both of them,' said Paddy.

The two men sat in a pub discussing their wives.

'My wife,' said one, 'does a lot of work for the church; collections, charity work and things like that.'

'My wife is a lay preacher,' remarked the other.

'Is she really?'

'Yeah. Every time we're having a lay she gives me a sermon.'

'Belfast Council is rotten,' observed a man who had imbibed rather freely.

'Ish that soo?' cooed his companion.

'Yesh. Do you see that cemetery? Well, they wouldn't let me bury my mother-in-law there.'

'Why not?'

'Shee wasn't dead,' came the sad reply.

It was the weekend outing for the men of a social club. Two of them sat in a pub each trying to write a postcard.

'I jesh wrote, "Love and miss you", my wife likes that.'

'I wrote "Norwich",' said the other.

'Norwich? Thest shilly.'

'S'not.'

'Whesh it mean?'

'Nickers off ready when I come home.'

A woman entered a bar and ordered two glasses of gin. 'Why two glasses,' asked the barman, 'when you're alone?'

'The other lady,' came the dignified reply, 'is lying outside.'

He wasn't a hard drinker. In fact he found it very easy.

She: 'I've no sympathy for a man who gets drunk every night.'

He: 'A man who gets drunk every night doesn't need sympathy.'

Wife: 'What do you mean by getting home at this hour.'

Husband: 'S'all right m'love. I hurried home 'cos I thought you might be lonely, but I shee your twin sister is staying with you.'

After his wife died, Harry had the habit of going down to the pub every night and having two glasses of whisky put in front of him. This, he explained was his way of remembering his wife. Every night he would have a drink with her, for old times' sake.

This went on for a year until one night he went into the pub and only ordered one drink.

'How come only one drink?' asked the barman.

'Oh, the wife has decided to give it up and save on the housekeeping money.'

The old drunk was well known to the police and was brought before a magistrate who also knew him.

'James Jordan,' said the magistrate with severity, 'you are charged with habitual drunkenness. Have you an excuse to offer for your offence?'

'Habitual thirst, your honour.'

'Shay, offisher, where am I?'
'You're on the corner of King Street and Oxford Street.'
'Never mind the street. What town am I in?'

Then there was the man who poured a measure of castor oil into his beer. He said it didn't do much for the taste of the beer but it gave him a better run for his money.

Don't drink and drive – it spills all over the steering wheel.

They were drunk after The Irish Hunt Dinner and wanted to leave.
'Wheresh the exit?'
The waiter pointed along the corridor.
'Turn to the right and go down two steps and you'll be in the front hall.'
Arm in arm, they staggered on, turned and fell down the lift shaft to the basement.
'Look Brendan. If that waiter thinks I'm going down the other step, he's crazy,' snorted Paddy.

The drunk tottered to the front door of his house and searched his pockets for the key. Pocket after pocket he tried until he came to his side trousers pocket which had a hole in it. Suddenly he exclaimed, 'Plums? Plums? When did I buy plums?'

'Mr Kelly, will you lend my husband your corkscrew?'
'Certainly Mrs O'Rourke, and I'll bring it over myself.'

The policeman stopped the little man who was running in the street and then let him go. The publican came pounding up to the policeman.

'Why didn't you stop that man?' he demanded.

'Well, Ian, he told me you were racing him for the price of a drink.'

'I certainly was. He didn't pay for it.'

The customer put two pounds on the bar counter and walked out. The barman put the money in his pocket and turned to find the accusing eye of the manager glaring at him.

'Would you believe that,' said the barman blandly. 'He leaves a two pound tip and doesn't pay for his drink!'

'I hope you're proud of yourself,' said the wife icily as her drunken husband tottered up the path of the house.

'I sure am,' replied her husband tipsily. 'I knew you would be standing there with a rolling pin in your hand, but I was brave, I came home anyway.'

The company under the command of Captain O'Thames was surrounded by the enemy under a tropical sun. Supplies were running low and a radio message was sent: 'Short of ammunition, no food or whisky.'

Headquarters radioed back: 'Any water?'

'This is no time to be thinking of washing,' replied Captain O'Thames.

The drunk staggered from the pub into his car and fumbled with his keys while a policeman watched him. The policeman went over and spoke to the driver.

'Excuse me sir, you're not thinking of driving that car the way you are?'

'Shertainly I am offisher, I'm too bloody drunk to walk.'

A man walked into a bar and ordered a martini. Before drinking it he carefully removed the olive from the stick and placed it in a small bottle. Then he ordered another martini and repeated the procedure. Two hours later, he was thoroughly sloshed and had got through thirty martinis in the same fashion. As he lifted the bottle and prepared to leave he slurred to the barman, 'My wife is expecting some guests for cocktails, and she sent me out for a bottle of olives.'

A man walked into a bar and asked for a glass of water. He drank it and walked out. The next day he was in again and asked for a glass of water, drank it and turned to go.

'Here,' complained the barman, 'you come in here, ask for a glass of water; drink it and then walk out ...'

'What do you want me to do,' cut in the man, 'stagger?'

Then there was the publican with two wooden legs whose pub went on fire. The local fire service saved the pub but he was burnt to the ground.

A drunk slowly staggering through the park came across a man doing press ups. He watched for a minute then mumbled, 'Scuse me old boy, but she's gone.'

A temperance preacher was delighted to hear a publican say that he always preferred a teetotaller to a moderate drinker, and asked him how he arrived at that conclusion.

'Well, it's like this,' said the publican. 'A moderate drinker comes into my bar, orders a glass of beer, and sits for an hour or more reading my papers and taking up space, but a teetotaller rushes into the off-licence section buys a couple of bottles of whisky and is gone in a flash.'

The two men sat in the pub drinking beer.

'You wonder,' said one drinker, lifting his glass, 'what the difference is between a pint of beer and a pint of water.'

'One pound ten pence,' replied the other glumly.

The two drunks staggered along the pier and one slipped and fell into the sea.

'Help, help!' shouted the man in the sea. 'I can't swim. I can't swim.'

'So what?' shouted back the drunk on the pier. 'Neither can I, but I'm not shouting about it.'

Never drink alone – always with a friend. That way you've always got someone to get you home.

'William,' she thundered, as she found an unopened bottle of whisky as she unpacked for a weekend camping, 'what's the meaning of this?'

'That's all right, my dear. I brought it along to stick a candle in it when it's empty.'

Two men sat in a pub knocking back beer after beer.

'You know, David, I think I'll buy this pub.'

'Wait until we've had a few more drinks,' said David, 'and I'll sell it to you.'

Many a drinking man puts his foot down only to find he hasn't got a leg to stand on.

'You have only heard one constable,' said the reveller. 'I want you to hear what the other constable has to say.'

'There wasn't another constable there,' pointed out the sergeant.

'You'll excuse me, but I saw him.'

'Yes, that's why you're here.'

First Drunk: 'Jesh passed a man who looks jesh like you.'

Second Drunk: 'Strange. Lesh go back and shee if it whash me.'

Passenger: 'Have I time for a drink?'

Bus Driver: 'Yes, sir.'

Passenger: 'Are you sure the bus won't go without me.'

Bus Driver: 'Quite sure. I'm coming with you.'

'How about another drink before we go?' John asked Stephen.

'Good idea,' replied Stephen as he sank into a drunken sleep.

'All I can say,' slurred John as he tried to focus on his sleeping drinking companion. 'You three are a right pair if I ever saw one.'

One drunk meeting another, 'You haven't got a pound have you?'

'Who told you?'

The Roman Catholic parish priest of a Belfast church was amazed to find two drunken Orange Protestants outside his window at two o'clock in the morning.

'What do you want?' he called.

'We want you to tell us if the Pope wants peace in Ulster,' shouted one.

'Look, come back in the morning and I'll discuss it when you're sober.'

'Sure when we're sober, we don't give a damn what the Pope wants.'

A man suffering from insomnia consulted an Irish doctor.

'Have a glass of whisky when you get into bed at night,' said the doctor.

'Will that make me sleep?' asked the patient.

'Well, if it doesn't, take another glass,' replied the doctor. 'If that doesn't make you sleep, take another glass and after the sixth glass you won't give a damn whether you sleep or not.'

The farewell party for the lone yachtsman had a high liquor content and when he set off he was quite inebriated. In a happy stupor he was suddenly aware of lights above him. He grabbed a loud-hailer and yelled, 'Shay, what the hell do you think you're doing? Can't you shee I'm under sail? I have the right of way.'

'Not this time you don't mate,' came a voice. 'This is a lighthouse.'

A judge and a friend went into a bar. The judge appeared undecided what to have.

'Have you tried brandy and ginger?' his friend asked.

'No,' replied the judge, 'but I've tried many who have.'

Here's to the girl who lives on the hill
What she won't do, her sister will
Here's to her sister.

Then there was the bottle of cheap brandy who went to the psychiatrist because he thought he was Napoleon.

The drunk staggered into a crowded pub, pushed his way through the customers and approached the bar. He elbowed his way past a woman to reach the bar where he belched loudly. The woman's companion turned to him angrily.

'How dare you push through like that and belch in front of my wife,' he said indignantly.

The drunk looked apologetic.

'I'm sorry to belch in front of your wife,' he blurted, 'I didn't realise it was her turn.'

A businessman was on his first visit to Los Angeles and was attending a business party. He was given a glass of the local wine and had just finished his drink when the furniture started to move about and the walls trembled.

'This is certainly a powerful drink,' he said to the host.

'Not really,' smiled the host, 'this happens to be an earthquake.'

The Yuppie was trying hard to chat up the barmaid.

'Tell me,' he said, 'do you have a thirst for knowledge.'

'Oh sure,' she replied. 'I can drink anything.'

As Dracula said when he was taking his bedtime drink, 'It really is thicker than water.'

The man was found unconscious in the street and was rushed to hospital. There, nurses found a note taped to his chest.

'Dear doctor, I am merely drunk. Just let me sleep it off and I will be all right. On no account remove my appendix, as you have twice done in the past.'

Here's to the girl in high heel shoes
Who smokes my cigs and drinks my booze
Who drinks and drinks
And never gets tight
Then goes and sleeps with her mother all night.

In a recent survey in which husbands were asked if they approved of their wives drinking:
48% said they preferred their wives not to drink;
12% said they preferred their wives to drink and
40% said they preferred to drink to their wives.

In a brewery a man fell into a vat of beer and had to swim around for twenty minutes before being rescued. He described it as a sobering experience.

An Ulsterman was so fond of drink that when he saw the sign – Drink Canada Dry – he emigrated.

Three drunks came out of a Belfast city centre pub and, on reaching the city hall took off their clothes and danced naked in the grounds.
They were chased by a patrol of the Ulster Defence Regiment. All three were caught. The first man was caught by the sergeant; the second man was caught by the corporal and the third man was caught by the privates.

The chief inspector waved a warning finger at the constable.

'Constable Jones, I've just received a report of your disgraceful behaviour at the station party last night,' stormed the chief inspector. 'Not only were you drunk, but while naked you pushed a wheelbarrow, with a naked man in it, around the yard. What exactly were you doing?'

'Well, you should know, sir,' replied the constable, 'you were in the wheelbarrow.'

The minister met the man in the street and greeted him with a kindly smile.

'Good morning, Peter,' beamed the minister. 'I was delighted to see you at choir practice last night.'

'Oh,' moaned Peter holding his head, 'is that where I was?'

A Scotsman dashed into a pub and ordered a double whisky.

'A double?' echoed the barman. 'What's wrong?'

'Mon, I had a narrow escape,' gasped the man, 'I was wiping ma brow with ma kilt and I was nearly arrested for indecent exposure.'

A man who caused a disturbance in the Crown and Anchor locked himself in a toilet.

The publican called the police who soon flushed him out.

The little man was sipping his drink at the bar when a tall, handsome soldier entered.

'Tickle your arse with a feather,' said the soldier to the pretty barmaid.

'What did you say?' demanded the barmaid.

'I said, "It's particularly nasty weather",' replied the soldier.

The little man thought this was a wonderful joke and decided to try it, so he tottered through the rain to another bar. Staggering up to the counter he paused, as he viewed the dragon-like barmaid, forgetting what to say he eventually blurted out, 'Stick the feather up your arse and it's raining like hell outside.'

Simon Potts, chained himself to the doors of the Dirty Duck and said he would stay there for twenty days in protest over the increased price of beer.

Brewery officials pleaded with him to call off the protest but he stated he was going to stick it out. He did so and was immediately arrested.

The policeman stopped the drunk and asked him where he was going.

'I'm coming home from a Noo Yearsh Eve party,' spluttered the drunk.

'Are you joking?' growled the policeman. 'New Year's Eve was three weeks ago.'

'I know, offisher,' answered the drunk. 'Thatsh why I reckon I better be getting home.'

If you drink like a fish – swim – don't drive.

A staggering drunk stopped a passer-by and asked the time. The passer-by looked at his watch and told him.

'I just can't work it out,' muttered the drunk, shaking his head. 'All night I've been getting different answers.'

As the drunk staggered home he was thinking how he could conceal his condition from his wife. He decided that when he got home he would sit and read a book: she would never suspect him of being drunk if he was reading.

When he reached home he slipped into the lounge and sat down. A minute later his wife came storming into the room.

'What do you think you're doing?' she asked.

'Just reading, dear, just reading,' answered the drunk.

'You're blind drunk again,' ranted his wife. 'Now close that suitcase and get to bed.'

When the drunk fell out of a window, his friend was the first to get to him.

'Were you hurt in the fall?' he asked.

'No, the fall didn't hurt a bit,' replied the drunk, 'but hitting the ground did.'

The man went into the hotel bedroom and saw a note on the table: Are You An Alcoholic? If So Telephone 23456. He did so and found it was an off-licence.

The angry wife wanted to know how her drunken husband had teeth marks on his forehead.
'I mushta bitten myshelf,' he said vaguely.
'How could you have bitten yourself up there?'
'Mebbe, I jumped,' the husband replied brightly.

The drunk gave the constable who was holding him up a hazy look, and asked, 'What am I here for?'
'Drinking,' said the sergeant at the desk.
'Oh good. I'll have a Guinness.'

A man, with both hands heavily bandaged, walked into a pub, ordered a pint of beer and asked the barmaid if she would hold the glass to his lips while he drank. The barmaid did this and also with several more pints. Finally the man asked where the toilet was. The barmaid looked at him in alarm then stammered, 'Oh, it's about a mile down the road.'

'Barman, did you give me a lemon?'
'No, sir.'
'Oh hell! I've just squeezed the canary into my gin.'

The drunk staggered into a late night cinema. The girl in the ticket office issued him a ticket for the stalls and he tottered in. A minute later he was out again – and bought another ticket. The girl served him with some surprise, but when he came back a third time she asked him what he was doing.

'Do you know that's the third ticket you've bought?'

'Shure I do,' replied the drunk. 'But as soon as I get inside the door, a big fella snatches them out of my hand and tears them up.'

The businessman telephoned his wife from a pub to say he had been delayed at the office.

'Don't tell me a pack of lies,' said the voice at the other end of the telephone. 'Get out of that pub immediately and come home ... This has been a recorded message.'

The chief fire officer looked miserable when the doctor told him he would have to give up drinking whisky.

'Replace your drinks with some substitute,' said the doctor, trying to be helpful. 'Every time you feel like drinking a whisky, eat an apple instead.'

The chief fire officer looked even more miserable.

'Sixty apples a day is going to play hell with my digestion,' he said sadly.

The two drunks were standing on a bridge looking down at the moon's reflection in the water.

First Drunk: 'What's that down there?'

Second Drunk: 'That's the moon.'
First Drunk: 'Well, if it's down there, where the hell are we?'

The drunk watched the policeman wading in the river. 'Whash yer looking for?' slurred the drunk.

'We're looking for a drowned man,' answered a policeman.

'Whash yer want one for?'

Drunk:　'Shay, call me a taxi.'
Barman: 'Certainly sir. You're a taxi.'

Same Drunk: 'Shay, call me a taxi.'
Officer:　　'My good man, I'm not a doorman, I am a naval officer.'
Same Drunk:　'Awright, then call me a boat, I gotta get home.'

He was doing his best to fit a key in the lock of the front door. After a time a man looked out of the window.

'Go away, you fool,' shouted the man at the window. 'You're trying to get into the wrong house.'

'Fool yourself!' yelled the drunk. 'You're looking out of the wrong window.'

'Now, constable,' said the inspector, 'just because a man is on his hands and knees in the middle of the road doesn't prove he's drunk.'

'No, sir, it doesn't. But this man thought he was a fireman and was trying to roll up the white line.'

A well-known Ulster preacher was in full flow at a meeting.

'Lightning will strike from the skies, the heavens will split open and flames will then envelope the earth and fire and brimstone will cover the land. All this will come on Judgement Day if you sinners will not give up the evil drink!'

A little man in the hall raised his hand.

'Yes?' thundered the preacher.

'Could you tell me,' asked the little man, 'if all this will happen before or after the pubs shut?'

Two duck hunters went for a morning shoot. One took a flask of hot coffee, the other a bottle of whisky. They sat all morning without seeing a duck, each drinking his own beverage.

Suddenly, a single solitary duck appeared in the sky. The coffee drinker took aim and fired but missed. The whisky drinker fired and the duck fell to earth like a stone.

'Boy, that was some shot,' said the coffee drinker. 'How did you manage it?'

'S'easy,' replied the whisky drinker. 'I jest fired into the middle of the flock.'

When a leading doctor announced that whisky, salads and sex were ingredients for a long life, some wit commented, 'Then if rabbits drank they would live for ever.'

A man was appearing in a London court on a charge of being drunk and disorderly and the magistrate asked the arresting officer to describe the defendant's behaviour.

'Well, sir,' said the policeman, 'at midnight I observed the defendant stagger across the road to the Houses of Parliament, place some coins in a letter box, peer up at Big Ben and exclaim, "Great. I've lost a stone and a bit".'

A man walked into a crowded pub, pushed his way to the bar and stood there twitching and waving his hands in the air. He kept this up for several minutes until a customer nudged him.

'What's wrong with you?' asked the customer.

'I'm suffering from yaws,' replied the man.

'Oh, what's yaws?'

The man stopped twitching, 'That's very kind of you. I'll have a large brandy.'

Meeting his friend Jim in a pub, Bill was surprised to see him knocking back whisky after whisky.

'I thought your doctor told you to stop all drinks,' said Bill.

'That's right,' replied Jim. 'That's exactly what I'm doing. Have you seen a single drink get past me?'

'You see, marriage hasn't changed him at all. He drinks as much as ever.'

'Yes, but he used to drink for pleasure, now it's from sorrow.'

'I drink brandy to cure my sciatica,' observed the seasoned drinker.

'Oh, I can give you a cure for sciatica,' chirped the young doctor.

'Shut up! I don't want to hear it!'

'Your glass is empty. Want another?' asked Pat.

'Now, why the hell would I be wanting two empty glasses?' snorted Mick.

'Oh, stop moaning,' said the drinking man to his wife. 'I was very quiet when I came home last night.'

'Yes, you were, but the two men who carried you upstairs weren't,' shouted his wife.

The drunk finished his tenth pint of beer and shouted he could lick any man in the house. A burly Irish navvy took him up on his boast and beat the living daylights out of him.

'God almighty,' said the drunk as he was helped to his feet, 'I said I could lick any man in the house – but that's no excuse for setting a gorilla on me.'

'I feel sorry for people who don't drink. When they wake up in the morning they know that's the best they're going to feel all day.'

Dean Martin

Sign in a pub: We have a special arrangement with the bank. They don't serve beer and we don't cash cheques.

The man had just staggered out of a pub when he was knocked down and robbed at the corner of Chichester Street and May Street. He tottered round to the police station to report the event.

'Where did this happen, sir?' asked the policeman.

'In Chic . . . Cic . . . Chick . . . in May Street.'

'I think you've had enough, sir,' said the barman.

'Noshings of the short.'

'Sir, you are blind drunk.'

'Let me thell you, I'm not blind drunk. I can shee very well. Look, there's a one-eyed cat coming into the bar.'

'Sir, that cat has two eyes and it's going out.'

The two women went into a bar for a drink.

'Two glasses of white wine,' ordered one. 'Make sure my glass is clean, last time you gave me a dirty glass.'

'Here you are, ladies,' said the waiter, returning with the wine. 'Now – which of you wanted the clean glass?'

A man stood at the bar looking miserable.

'Anything wrong?' asked one of the regulars.

'I'm lonely,' confided the man.

'Well, cheer up,' said the regular. 'Let me buy you a drink.'

'Thanks,' said the sad man, 'I'll have a double brandy.'

'Christ mate,' said the regular, 'no wonder you're lonely.'

Liam met Paddy in the street. Paddy was carrying a crate of Guinness and two bottles of whisky.

'Going to a party?' asks Liam.

'No,' replied Paddy, 'movin' house.'

'Good evening Father,' said Patrick, trying not to sway too much.

'Good evening Patrick,' replied the priest wondering how long the drunk could stand.

'Glad to see you Father, 'cos I wanted to ask you a question,' said Patrick, backing to a wall.

'Well, Patrick, what's your question?'

'Tell me, Father, what causes arthritis?'

'Ah, Patrick,' lectured the priest. 'Arthritis is caused by wild living, over-eating, but most of all by too much alcohol. How long have you had arthritis?'

'I don't have arthritis,' grinned the drunk, 'but I read in the paper today that the Pope has.'

A drunk staggered into a police station with a duck stuck to his head.

'Can I help you?' asked the duty sergeant.

'Yes,' said the duck, 'get this man off my feet.'

A Salvation Army girl walked into a pub carrying a bundle of papers.

'How about a War Cry?' she asked.

'Certainly,' hooted a drunk. 'Up The Black Watch!'

It was the same Salvation Army girl who asked the habitual drunk what made him drink.

'Why, miss,' smiled the drunk, 'nothing makes me do it. I'm a volunteer.'

There is a pub where the beer is so weak the customers never get drunk – they just get water-logged.

A millionaire filled his swimming pool with gin to make accidental drowning impossible. The deeper you sank the higher you got.

The man walked into a pub and said to the barman, 'I have a terrible cold.'

'Well,' said the barman, 'go home and drink a bottle of whisky.'

'Will the whisky cure the cold?' asked the customer.

'It may not cure your cold, but it'll keep the germs so bloody drunk they won't bother you.'

The Scotsman was served a pint of beer which had a very thick head on it.

'Tell me,' said the Scotsman to the barman, 'could you squeeze a double Scotch into this glass?'

The barman looked at the glass.

'Certainly,' he said.

'Right then,' said the Scotsman. 'You better fill up the hole with beer.'

When the young couple returned from holiday, they were pleased to find a note from some friends stating they had left a gift in the milk rack.

Eagerly the couple went to the milk rack, only to find another note – this time from the milkman, thanking them for the bottle of Scotch.

He had been introduced to his favourite film actress and was completely enchanted. Her hair was as blonde as he had dreamed, her eyes sparkled and she was beautiful.

'A drink?' he ventured. 'Port or sherry?'

'Oh, sherry by all means,' the angel replied. 'Sherry to me is the nectar of the Gods. Just looking at it gives me the anticipation of a heavenly thrill and when I experience the fragrance I am lifted on the wings of joy. When I taste it my entire body glows and I am carried to another world. On the other hand,' she continued, 'port makes me fart.'

Willie Boggs, from Ballymena, was very drunk as he staggered into the bus station to get a bus to Larne. Just as he got into the station he collided with a young lady and she fell on her back with him on top of her.

'Just what do you think you're doing?' she demanded.

'Miss, it's all right,' replied Willie, 'I'm just going to Larne.'

'Aye, well, you can get off,' the girl shouted at him. 'You're not going to Larne on me.'

The two women were in the pub and had finished their drinks.

'Are you having another one?' one woman asked.

'No,' replied the other, 'it's just the way my coat's buttoned.'

The husband staggered into the hall of his home after having a few drinks too many.

His wife immediately set about him, 'If this were the first time, Nigel, I could forgive you, but you came home in exactly the same state in August twenty years ago when England won a test match.'

The girl sitting on the bar stool was shapely and tempting. Naturally, she aroused the interest of the playboy at the other end of the bar. He smiled at her. Then he winked. When this failed, he tried his best leer. Just then the bartender – sixteen stone of tanned muscle – leaned over the bar and said, 'Look, mate, that's my wife, so cut out the funny business.'

'Funny business?' replied the flustered playboy. 'I don't know what you're talking about. I just dropped in for a cool drink. Give me a piece of beer.'

Two inebriated men stood at the bar near closing time.

'I've an idea,' said one, 'lesh have one more drink and go and find us shum girls.'

'Naw,' replied the other. 'I've more than I can handle at home.'

'Great,' gurgled the ideas man, 'then lesh have one more drink and then go to your place.'

He offered her a Scotch and sofa and she reclined.

A man staggered up the path to the front door of a house and tried to get the key into the lock. A watching policeman approached him, 'Excuse me sir, are you sure this is your house?'

'Shertainly,' said the drunk, 'and if you just open the door f' me, I'll prove it to you.'

The policeman slipped the key into the lock and the door swung open.

'Mon in,' said the drunk. 'See that television set? Thash mine. See that music centre? Thash mine too. Mon upstairs.'

The drunk crawled up the stairs to the first floor and pushed open a door.

'Thish is my bedroom,' he announced. 'See that bed? Thash my bed. See the woman in bed? Thash my wife. And see the man lying beside her?'

'Yes,' said the policeman suspiciously.

'Thash me!'

'How many drinks does it take to make you dizzy?'
'Five or six,' she retorted, 'and don't call me Dizzy.'

The wife was complaining about her husband going out every night to the pub. So one evening he took her along to the local.

'What'll you have?' he asked.

'The same as you,' she replied.

The husband ordered two pints of bitter and took a long drink from his glass. His wife watched him then took a sip from her glass and immediately spat it out.

'I don't know how you drink this stuff,' she said, 'it tastes terrible.'

'There you are,' cried the husband, 'and you think I'm out enjoying myself every night!'

Then there was the film star who claimed to have the tightest security in the world – his bodyguards were always drunk.

'I would like your opinion of my new cocktail,' said the barman.

'It's worthless,' replied the drinker.

'I know,' persisted the barman, 'but I'd like it anyhow.'

The man staggered out of the pub and crashed into a lamp standard. Rubbing his head he then walked against a pillar box and from that banged into a telephone booth. At this stage he tottered into a doorway, curled up muttering, 'I might as well stay here 'till the parade passes.'

The two drunks were in a car which was speeding along the road, just missing other cars by inches.

'For God's sake, look where you're driving,' cried one drunk.

'Am I driving?' asked the other drunk. 'I thought you were.'

A brewery worker fell into a vat of beer and was drowned. The manager went to tell the widow. Naturally she was very upset and started to weep.

'Did he suffer much?' she sobbed.

'I don't think so,' replied the manager, 'he got out twice to go to the gents!'

A drunk got on a train and told the ticket collector he'd bought a ticket but couldn't find it.

'It doesn't matter,' said the collector, 'I'm sure you paid.'

'But it does matter,' exclaimed the drunk. 'Without the ticket I don't know where I'm going!'

The lecturer took a wriggling worm from a jar and dropped it into a glass of whisky. The worm wriggled for a few seconds then died.

'Well,' said the lecturer to the class, 'after seeing that demonstration what are your conclusions?'

'If you're troubled with worms, drink whisky,' answered a student.

As the young Salvation Army girl walked through the pub selling copies of War Cry, a drunk grabbed her by the arm.

'Tell me, dear,' he asked, 'do you people save loose women?'

'We certainly do,' replied the girl with a smile.'

'Good,' said the drunk. 'Save me one for next Saturday night.'

'**I** exercise extreme self control. I never drink anything stronger than gin before breakfast.'

W.C. Fields

The two men promised to meet in the same bar on New Year's Eve the following year. So, one year later one of them walked in and sure enough there was his friend on a stool.

'I never thought when we left this bar last year I'd see you here today,' he said.

'Who left?' hiccuped his friend on the stool.

'**I**s your husband on sick leave?'
'Yes, he's suffering from bottle fatigue.'

Three drunks staggering down the High Street were apprehended by the police. They conferred together and decided to give false names made up from the shops in the street.

'What's your name?' the policeman asked the first man.

'Mark Spencer,' replied the drunk.

'Your name?' the policeman continued.

'John Smith,' smiled the second drunk.

'And your name, sir?' asked the policeman.

'Er . . er . . Ken Tucky Fried Chicken.'

'Why do you buy two drinks and then drink them yourself?' asked the barman.

'Well,' said the drinker, 'the first drink makes me feel a new man and it's only right I buy him a drink too.'

Desmond and Michael had downed quite a few before playing in the club championship and as Desmond was about to tee off he whispered to Michael, 'I can see three balls.'

'Well, hit the middle one,' ordered Michael.

Desmond took his stance, had a mighty swing, missed the ball and landed on his back.

'What's the matter?' hissed Michael. 'Didn't I tell you to hit the middle ball?'

'Yes, but you didn't tell me to use the middle club,' replied Desmond.